Eating Disorders

By Jane Bingham

Health Consultant: John G. Samanich, M.D.

Gareth Stevens
Publishing

A WEEKLY READER COMPANY

Please visit our web site at www.garethstevens.com.
For a free color catalog describing Gareth Stevens
Publishing's list of high-quality books, call
1-800-542-2595 (USA) or 1-800-387-3178 (Canada).
Gareth Stevens Publishing's fax: 1-877-542-2596

Library of Congress Cataloging in Publication Data

Bingham, Jane
  Eating disorders / Jane Bingham. — North American ed.
    p. cm. — (Emotional health issues)
  Originally published: London : Wayland, 2008.
  Includes bibliographical references and index.
  ISBN-10: 0-8368-9200-3
  ISBN-13: 978-0-8368-9200-0 (lib. bdg.)
  1. Eating disorders. I. Title.
RC552.E18B512   2009
616.85'26—dc22   2008000825

The information in this book is not intended to substitute for professional medical or psychological care. The case studies are based on real experiences, but the names are fictitious. All people in the photos are models except where a caption specifically names an individual.

This North American edition first published in 2009 by
Gareth Stevens Publishing
A Weekly Reader® Company
1 Reader's Digest Road
Pleasantville, NY 10570-7000 USA

This U.S. edition copyright © 2009 by Gareth Stevens, Inc.
Original edition copyright © 2008 by Wayland. First published in Great Britain in 2008
by Wayland, 338 Euston Road, London NW1 3BH, United Kingdom.

Series Editor: Nicola Edwards   Consultant: Peter Evans
Designer: Alix Wood   Picture Researcher: Kathy Lockley

Gareth Stevens Managing Editor: Lisa M. Herrington
Gareth Stevens Senior Editor: Barbara Bakowski
Gareth Stevens Creative Director: Lisa Donovan

Photo credits: Mark Baigent/Alamy Images: 4, 15; Bubbles Photolibrary/Alamy Images: title page, 7, 22, 27, 43; Le Studio/AgenceImages/Jupiter Images 12; CLEO Photo/Alamy Images: 20; Enigma/Alamy Images: 23; David J. Green/Alamy Images: Cover, 10; Sally & Richard Greenhill/Alamy Images: 21, 35; Charles Gullung/zefa/Corbis: 17; Angela Hampton/Alamy Images: 38; John Henley/Corbis: 19; Jack Hollingsworth/Corbis: 32; Crispin Hughes/Photofusion Picture Library: 39; Image100/Corbis: 13; Image Source/Corbis: 26; Ghislain & Marie David de Lossy/Image Bank/Getty Images: 16; Lisa Peardon/Taxi/Getty Images: 45; Jose Luis Pelaez, Inc/Corbis: 8; Photofusion Picture Library/Alamy Images: 9; Pixland/Corbis: 44; Ed Quinn/Corbis: 28; Rex Features: 33; Gary Roberts/Rex Features: 25; TWPhoto/Corbis: 37; Penny Tweedie/Alamy Images: 30: Wayland Archive: 14, 31, 36, 40, 42; Heiko Wolfraum/DPA/PA Photos: 18; Jerome Yeats/Alamy Images: 34; David Young-Wolff/Alamy Images: 41

Printed in China
1 2 3 4 5 6 7 8 9 10 09 08

Contents

Words that appear in **boldface** type are in the glossary on page 46.

Introduction

K im's favorite treat used to be going out for pizza, but now she can't even bear the thought of it. Even though she is hungry all the time, she feels she can't allow herself to eat. When she looks in the mirror, she is convinced she is fat. She hates the way her family and her friends are always urging her to gain weight. Kim feels lonely, exhausted, and scared. She also feels that the only way to stay in control of her life is to be thin.

Anorexia and bulimia

Kim has **anorexia nervosa**, usually called anorexia. People who have this condition—known as anorexics—have an overwhelming need to be thin. They see themselves as overweight, and they deliberately **fast**, allowing themselves to eat only tiny amounts of food. Many anorexics also put themselves through a punishing program of intensive exercise to prevent any weight gain.

Eating disorders among teens have increased dramatically in recent decades.

Anorexia is one of a range of eating disorders that also includes **bulimia nervosa**, known as bulimia. Bulimics alternate between frantic **bingeing**, when they eat huge amounts of food, and drastic **purging**, when they empty their bodies of everything they've eaten. Bulimics purge by making themselves vomit or by using **laxatives**. After a bingeing session, some bulimics also have a period of excessive fasting and exercise.

Unlike anorexics, who are significantly underweight, most bulimics are of normal or above-normal weight. Both groups, however, have a serious disorder. Although anorexia and bulimia can affect people of all ages, these disorders are most common among girls between the ages of 11 and 18. However, a growing number of teenage boys are developing eating disorders, too.

Find out more

This book gives you the facts about anorexia, bulimia, **binge-eating disorder**, and **compulsive eating disorder**. You will learn about the destructive physical and psychological effects. The following chapters describe why teenagers may develop difficulties with eating. The book also offers advice on seeking help and shows how people can recover from eating disorders and lead healthy lives.

It's a fact: eating disorders

- About 8 million teenagers in the United States have an eating disorder.

- Four out of every 10 Americans have had an eating disorder or have known someone with an eating disorder.

- Approximately 10 percent of teenagers with eating disorders are boys.

- Almost 90 percent of people with eating disorders are from 12 to 25 years old.

- More than half of teenage girls are, or think they should be, on diets. About 3 percent of these teens eventually develop an eating disorder.

- Fewer than half of people with eating disorders receive treatment.

- Many people with eating disorders have other mental health or emotional problems, such as **depression** or drug and alcohol abuse.

Chapter 1: What is anorexia?

How does anorexia start? What happens when a teenager develops this serious eating disorder? This chapter describes the early stages of anorexia and explores the feelings and reactions of people as difficulties with eating take over their lives.

Deciding to diet

Anorexia usually starts with a decision to lose weight. There can be many reasons behind this choice (see Chapter 5). Whatever the reasons, the basic decision is the same: A teenager is unhappy with the way she or he looks. The teen decides to make some changes by losing weight.

He or she may cut back on fattening foods, stop eating snacks between meals, or simply reduce portion sizes. This behavior can go unnoticed by others. Sometimes family members and friends praise the teen for losing weight and compliment his or her slimmer shape.

Most teenagers don't diet for long. They soon become hungry and tired and decide to give up. In a few cases, though, teenagers persist and even intensify their dieting efforts. They become at risk of developing anorexia.

Very few anorexics begin with the intention of losing a lot of weight. Once they start to drop pounds, though, they feel a powerful need to continue.

It's a fact:

anorexia

- Anorexia commonly starts in the early teens to mid-teens. The highest rate is in girls ages 13 to 19.

- In the United States, approximately one in 100 girls and young women has anorexia. About one in 1,000 boys and young men has anorexia.

- Some studies report that about 5 percent of anorexics die from complications of the eating disorder.

It can be difficult for families to recognize the early stages of anorexia. Many parents believe that their teenager is just on a short-term diet.

Taking control

These teens discover that when they take control of what they eat, they feel much more in control of the rest of their lives. They have a sense of achievement as they watch their weight go down. They also feel proud of their willpower as they manage to force themselves to overcome their feelings of hunger.

As they start to lose weight, some teenagers feel the need to test themselves more and more. At the same time, they become increasingly critical of their bodies and decide that they need to lose more weight.

At this stage, their dieting usually becomes much more severe. They may start to skip meals and drastically reduce the amount of food they eat.

Conflicts with concerned family members and friends arise. Anorexia has begun in earnest.

In focus: teenage dieting

There is a growing trend for teenagers to go on diets. In a recent survey, 40 percent of American teenagers reported that they dieted either "sometimes" or "very often."

Although the majority of teens who diet don't develop anorexia, they are in danger of damaging their health. Cutting down on food during the teenage years can be especially harmful. Young people's bodies are growing quickly, and teens need regular supplies of a variety of **nutrients**. In the short term, dieting can leave teenagers feeling weak and tired. It can also have lasting negative effects on their health.

Avoiding eating

Anorexics soon learn strategies that allow them to eat as little as possible without attracting notice. Anorexic teenagers often try to avoid eating with friends and family. The teens may cut up food into little pieces and eat very slowly. They may simply push their food around on their plates. Some anorexics try to get rid of food secretly when nobody is looking. Sometimes anorexics make a show of eating normal amounts of food at a family meal but severely restrict their intake for the rest of the day. All of these strategies for avoiding eating can disguise the problem until the disorder is well advanced.

Strategies to avoid eating can also cause the teenager to become increasingly isolated. When young people skip meals with their family and friends, they miss out on valuable opportunities to socialize. Even when they are present at a meal, they cannot relax and enjoy the company. They are constantly on their guard to keep others from noticing how little they are eating.

Thinking of food

As anorexics try to avoid eating, they find themselves thinking more and more about food. Sometimes people with anorexia become preoccupied with counting **calories**—the units of energy contained in food. Many anorexics memorize the number of calories contained in each type of food. Some anorexics weigh out portions of food so that they can more

As anorexia develops, many teens avoid any situation where they have to eat with their friends. This means they miss out on a lot of fun.

Many young people with anorexia take a great interest in food and prepare large meals for their families. Anorexics, however, usually eat none of the food they cook.

precisely calculate the number of calories they will consume.

Even though they are eating very little food themselves, many teenagers with anorexia take a great interest in cooking. They may start to read recipe books, or they may cook elaborate family meals that they don't eat themselves. Even as they are eating less and less food, they may urge others to eat more. All of these activities reflect an unhealthy relationship with food.

In focus: cutting calories

Teenagers need to consume a large number of calories each day because their bodies are growing and developing quickly. An active teenage girl should consume about 2,200 calories daily. Teenage boys need about 2,800 calories each day.

Most anorexics consume fewer than 1,000 calories a day. By drastically reducing the number of calories they consume, they put their health in serious danger.

Feeling fat

Anorexics have a distorted **body image**. An anorexic boy may look in the mirror and see himself as fat even though he is really dangerously thin. An anorexic girl may become so scared of being overweight that she sees unwanted fat on her thighs, even though she is seriously underweight.

Exercising too much

Many people with anorexia push themselves to exercise more than they did before. They want to burn off all the calories they have consumed. Some teenagers who are developing anorexia start to walk faster. They may avoid sitting down and relaxing, preferring instead to stand up or pace about.

As anorexia takes hold, some people increase their level of activity dramatically. They may begin doing a lot of sit-ups or swim many laps in a pool.

Teenagers with anorexia do not see their bodies as others do. When they look in the mirror, they see themselves as overweight. They remain critical of their bodies and continue to push themselves to lose more pounds.

These punishing workouts can take up large amounts of time, making teenagers with anorexia even more isolated from their friends. Some anorexics who overexercise also have trouble keeping up with schoolwork. Excessive exercise can leave them feeling exhausted and weak.

Purging and pills

Some anorexics don't just restrict their food intake. They also purge their bodies of any food they do eat. They do this by making themselves vomit or by taking laxatives. This kind of behavior also occurs among people with bulimia (see Chapter 2). It can be extremely damaging to the anorexic's health, especially when he or she is dangerously underweight.

Anorexics may also use other methods to keep their weight low. Some teens with anorexia smoke cigarettes or drink alcohol to reduce their appetite. They may take diet pills, hoping to speed up the rate at which their body burns calories. Some anorexics take **diuretic** pills. Diuretics make a person urinate frequently, so the body loses a lot of water. The loss of fluids causes temporary weight loss. Taking diuretics can lead to **dehydration**, a serious condition in which the body lacks enough water to function properly.

In focus: family and friends

It can be very distressing for family and friends to watch someone they love experience anorexia. In this situation, many people feel tempted to urge the anorexic to eat, but their pleas usually have negative results. Mealtimes can become a battleground. As the anorexic becomes more determined not to eat, family and friends grow increasingly angry and frustrated.

Mental health experts say that the most important thing that family members and friends can do is to make sure that the anorexic teenager receives professional help (see Chapter 6). Meanwhile, they should try to keep mealtimes as stress-free as possible.

See page 47 for a list of useful web sites for the families and friends of people who are experiencing difficulties with eating.

Feeling hungry and tired

People with anorexia wage a constant battle with hunger and exhaustion. Without much food in their stomachs, they suffer from gnawing hunger pains. They also experience weakness and exhaustion because they are not providing their bodies with enough nutrients and energy.

In this state of weakness, even the smallest physical effort becomes much harder. Yet despite their exhaustion, many anorexics exercise excessively. Anorexics often have trouble sleeping, too, making their feelings of tiredness even more extreme.

Seeking perfection

Many anorexics are **perfectionists**. They are used to pushing themselves to do their best. When they decide to diet, they bring their usual determination and willpower to the task. Sadly, they soon become locked into the misery of anorexia.

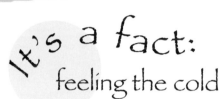

It's a fact: feeling the cold

Besides feeling hungry and tired, anorexics feel cold most of the time. There are two reasons for this effect:

- Anorexics lack the usual body covering of fat to keep them warm.

- Anorexics have poor **circulation**. As a result of fasting, their bodies do not receive enough energy to keep functioning normally. The heart reacts by slowing down and pumping blood around the body less vigorously. As a result, anorexics find it very hard to keep warm, and they usually have icy fingers and toes.

Even as these teens exhaust themselves by dieting and exercising excessively, they try very hard to keep up with their other activities. They set higher and higher standards for themselves. Many anorexics push themselves to excel at school, in spite of feeling weak and tired all the time. This effort is made even more difficult because anorexia affects their ability to think and concentrate.

People with anorexia often have trouble sleeping. They may wake up frequently during the night, no matter how tired they feel.

In focus: compulsive behavior

Anorexia and other difficulties with eating may be forms of obsessive or compulsive behavior. People who have **obsessive-compulsive disorder** (OCD) feel that their world is out of control, so they develop ways to try to control it.

Obsessive-compulsive disorder can take many forms. People with OCD may be obsessed by what they eat or by being extremely tidy, for example. They establish certain "rules" that they try to follow. By rigidly following these personal rules, people with OCD feel calmer and more in control. Breaking the rules can make them frightened and panicky.

OCD is a serious mental illness. Treatment often includes individual or family therapy and sometimes medication.

Losing concentration

One of the symptoms of anorexia is a loss of concentration. Besides feeling hungry, cold, and miserable, anorexics find that their mental abilities are not as sharp as they used to be.

Many teenage anorexics spend hours slaving over their homework but have trouble focusing on the task. Their grades frequently slip. Meanwhile, all those hours of hard work and study have the effect of cutting the teens off from their friends and family.

Feeling sad and isolated

Along with the physical symptoms of anorexia, teens with the disorder can experience negative **psychological** effects. They may become anxious, sad, moody, or irritable. Some anorexics feel despair at their inability to cope with the demands of their lives.

Many teenagers with anorexia stop taking part in social events they used to enjoy. They spend more and more time alone, feeling isolated and cut off from others.

Teenagers who have an eating disorder can feel very lonely. They may think that no one else understands what they are going through.

CASE STUDY

Kate was a quiet, hard-working girl who always did well at school. She had a small group of good friends. Then, when she was 13, the situation began to change. Her friends started ignoring her and hanging around with boys. One day Kate heard them laughing at her.

Kate blamed herself for doing something wrong. She had gained some weight recently, and she didn't like the way her body had changed. She decided to go on a diet. In just a few weeks, she lost 6 pounds (3 kilograms). Kate's parents started urging her to eat. Meanwhile, life at school was becoming worse. She was struggling to keep up with her work and felt even more cut off from her friends.

Kate made up her mind to eat even less. At least, she thought, dieting was something she could do really well. She also set a strict exercise schedule and got up early every morning to work out. As her weight continued to drop, Kate became more withdrawn. She stopped expecting anyone to understand her. Instead, she concentrated all her attention on her one goal—losing as much weight as she could.

Often, anorexics come into conflict with the people around them—especially when they are urged to eat. They may feel lonely and misunderstood as they struggle with the eating disorder. Some teenage anorexics feel so isolated and desperate that they have thoughts of suicide. A few anorexics make the tragic decision to kill themselves.

As anorexia takes hold, teens have difficulty concentrating on schoolwork. Tasks that once seemed easy take much longer to complete.

Chapter 2: What is bulimia?

Bulimia involves a pattern of behavior known as bingeing and purging. Bulimics eat a large amount of food in a short time. Then they empty their stomachs instead of digesting the food. This chapter describes the typical experiences of teenagers with bulimia.

Craving food

People with bulimia experience cravings for food. They respond by eating a large amount of food within a short time. Bulimics may eat large quantities of "regular" food, such as cereal. More commonly, however, people with bulimia binge on the sorts of foods that they don't usually allow themselves to eat, such as cupcakes, cookies, or ice cream.

People may develop bulimia for a variety of reasons (see Chapter 5). However, research has shown that bulimia often develops after people have dieted rigorously and eliminated certain foods. After a period of feeling hungry all the time, people find themselves desperately craving food—especially the treats they've forced themselves to give up. Once they give in to the urge to taste the "forbidden" foods, they find that they are unable to stop eating.

All people have occasional cravings for foods they like, but bulimics can't control those feelings. They find it hard to stop eating certain foods.

Feeling disgusted

Binges may last as long as two hours. These episodes often leave bulimics feeling uncomfortably full. Once their craving has eased, they are left with powerful feelings of shame and disgust. They are furious with themselves for breaking the rules of their diet. Bulimics are also horrified at the thought of the weight they will gain. Filled with disgust at their loss of control, they decide to take drastic action to get rid of as much food as possible before it can be digested. They purge by vomiting or by using laxatives.

It is possible to keep bulimia secret for a long time. Teenagers are often unaware that one of their friends is bulimic.

It's a fact: bulimia

- Bulimia affects 1 to 3 percent of middle and high school girls. The exact number of bulimics is unknown, though, because many people keep their condition secret.

- Bulimia commonly begins in the mid-teens.

- About 10 percent of bulimics are male. Current research indicates that bulimia is on the rise among boys and young men.

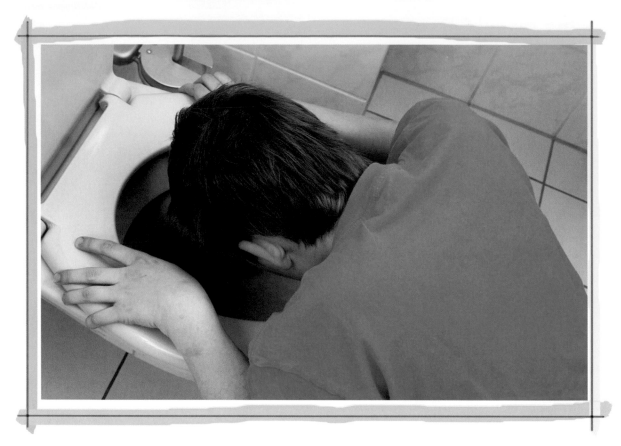

Purging

Bulimics can teach themselves how to vomit their food. Some make themselves sick by sticking their fingers down their throat. Others may use an instrument, such as a spoon handle, to stimulate the **gag reflex**. The practice of deliberately vomiting can lead to a range of medical problems (see Chapter 4).

Many bulimics also use laxatives in an attempt to expel as much food as possible from their bodies. Frequent use of laxatives can result in permanent damage to the kidneys and other internal organs. It can also cause heart problems and even heart failure.

Many bulimics try to empty their stomachs by vomiting. Frequent intentional vomiting can have serious side effects. (To find out more, see Chapter 4.)

Starting a vicious cycle

Once bulimics have started to binge and purge, they become caught up in a cycle of disordered eating. They indulge in regular overeating sessions and then try to empty the contents of their stomachs.

In some extreme cases, bulimics completely lose control of their eating habits. They enter into a pattern of compulsive behavior in which they overeat at every meal. The overeating is immediately followed by feelings of disgust. The bulimics purge, and the destructive cycle begins again.

Keeping secrets

Most bulimics feel intensely ashamed of their behavior and try to keep it hidden from others. They usually binge in secret and sneak to the bathroom to purge. This secretive behavior can have a bad effect on their relationships. An atmosphere of distrust often builds up as family and friends begin to suspect that the teenager has an eating disorder.

In this climate of distrust and suspicion, a bulimic teenager can become increasingly withdrawn. Many bulimics feel that they have to struggle with their problem alone. They feel scared and isolated as they try to cope with a problem that is spiraling out of control.

CASE STUDY

After six weeks on a very strict diet, Jo was miserable. She was constantly hungry and thinking of food. Then, one day, something snapped. Jo found herself raiding the refrigerator, eating a whole tub of ice cream. She followed by devouring six doughnuts and a box of cookies. She felt as if something had taken over her body, and she simply could not stop stuffing herself.

When she finally finished, Jo felt sick and deeply ashamed. How could she have broken her diet and lost her self-control? She desperately wanted to get rid of the hated food. She crept to the bathroom and locked the door.

Jo soon became an expert at getting rid of food. Within a few weeks, she was bingeing and purging every day. Jo spent all her money on cookies and candy, and she carefully hid the evidence of her binges. She had entered the secret, and often devastating, cycle of bulimia.

When teenagers try to hide their struggles with bulimia, a tense situation can develop at home. Worried parents often become suspicious and even angry. Teens can feel resentful and alone.

Chapter 3: *Bingeing and overeating*

Anorexia and bulimia are not the only problems people have with eating. Many teenagers feel compelled to eat too much. Just like anorexics and bulimics, they have an unhealthy relationship with food and are putting their health at risk.

Binge-eating disorder

People with binge-eating disorder frequently eat huge amounts of food at a single session. Just like bulimics, binge eaters have powerful cravings for certain foods. When they act on those cravings, they feel that they lose control. Afterward, binge eaters experience powerful feelings of disgust, shame, and remorse. Unlike bulimics, however, people with binge-eating disorder do not purge.

Most teens with binge-eating disorder are overweight, but some are not. They try to keep their condition secret, and they struggle to cope on their own.

Many overweight teens experience teasing. They may be more likely to turn to food for comfort and eventually develop binge-eating disorder.

People with binge-eating disorder may choose foods that are high in fat and sugar. After a binge, they feel guilty.

Compulsive eating disorder

People with compulsive eating disorder eat large amounts of food even when they are full. This abnormal eating behavior may happen regularly, or it may come and go in cycles. Compulsive eating disorder usually develops as a way of coping with stress, as people use food to comfort themselves. They may see eating as a way to escape their troubles, but the habit can rapidly spiral out of control, along with their weight.

Teenagers who overeat on a regular basis can easily get locked into a vicious cycle. They feel unhappy because they are overweight, so they eat compulsively to make themselves feel better. However, this behavior makes them feel worse and leads to more compulsive eating.

People with compulsive eating disorder put their health at risk (see page 23). Being seriously overweight can cause a wide range of physical problems. Compulsive overeaters often have low **self-esteem** and may experience depression.

CASE STUDY

When Dan was nine, his parents divorced. After his dad moved out, his mom became depressed. Dan tried to spend a lot of time with her. They often ate as they watched TV at home. By age 12, Dan was overweight.

At school, the students called Dan names. In gym class, he was always the last player picked for teams. To make himself feel better, Dan turned to food. Even when he wasn't hungry he was comforted by the taste and the feel of food in his mouth.

Eventually, Dan no longer recognized whether he was hungry; he knew only that he desperately wanted to eat. He hated the way he looked and felt, but he didn't know how to stop his powerful cravings for food.

Dan felt alone in his struggle. He didn't know that millions of other Americans also have compulsive eating disorder.

Chapter 4: *Symptoms and effects*

What are the signs that a person is developing an eating disorder? Sometimes a dramatic change in weight alerts others to the problem, although many bulimics do not experience weight loss or gain. Other changes can also provide clues to disordered eating patterns. People with eating disorders often experience changes in their behavior. The physical and psychological effects of eating disorders can be extremely damaging—and sometimes irreversible.

Changes in behavior

One of the first warning signs of an eating disorder may be a change in behavior. Most teenagers with anorexia or bulimia become more secretive and withdrawn. In the early stages of anorexia, they begin skipping meals and make excuses to eat very little. They usually avoid certain foods (especially high-calorie items). They may even announce a dramatic change in food preferences, such as a switch to a vegetarian diet. People who are developing bulimia will start making trips to the bathroom shortly after meals.

When teenagers refuse to eat foods they used to enjoy, they may be developing anorexia.

Anorexics often become hyperactive, rarely sitting still. They may exercise vigorously, often for hours each day. Other signs include irritability, moodiness, sleeplessness, and a deliberate avoidance of social occasions, especially those that involve food.

Anorexia: the physical signs

As anorexia develops, several physical changes occur. The most obvious effect is a dramatic weight loss. Other physical signs are thinning hair, brittle nails, and dry, flaky skin. These changes take place when the body receives too few nutrients to function properly. It is unable to replace skin, nail, and hair cells efficiently.

Anorexics often have red or purplish hands and feet because of poor circulation. They usually grow fine, downy hair on the face, arms, stomach, and back. This fine hair, known as **lanugo**, is a means of preserving heat as the body temperature drops.

In focus: symptoms and effects of bingeing and overeating

Compulsive overeaters are overweight, and teenagers who binge usually have weight problems, too. These groups of teenagers can experience a wide range of health problems caused by being overweight. They may experience back pain and problems with their joints. Excessive eating can damage their digestive systems. Being overweight puts excessive strain on the heart and lungs, too.

Teens who overeat compulsively are at risk of developing **diabetes**. People with that disease have high levels of blood sugar, which can lead to serious complications. High blood sugar levels directly affect the eyes, kidneys, and nervous system. Overweight teenagers are setting the stage for many health problems later in life.

Being overweight puts the body under a lot of strain. Severely overweight people are at risk of developing serious health problems.

Bulimia: the physical signs

Many teenagers with bulimia have a puffy-looking face with swollen cheeks. Whenever a person vomits, the **salivary glands** produce large amounts of saliva. In bulimics who vomit regularly, these glands become enlarged, causing "chipmunk cheeks." Bulimics often have broken **blood vessels** in the eyes, from the strain of frequent vomiting.

Many bulimics have damaged, decayed, or discolored teeth. When they vomit, their mouths fill with acid from the stomach. Contact with the powerful acid wears away the enamel that protects teeth.

People who have bulimia can also experience swelling of the stomach, ankles, and fingers because of a lack of **protein** in the body. This deficiency is a side effect of the regular use of laxatives, which strips the body of many valuable nutrients.

Medical effects

Some serious physical changes underlie the signs and symptoms of eating disorders. Many of the effects of an eating disorder can be reversed once normal eating is resumed. However, some types of damage are permanent. Medical professionals stress the importance of seeking help for an eating disorder as soon as possible.

Circulation problems

Most anorexics have low blood pressure and poor circulation. In response to the reduced amount of energy delivered through food, the anorexic's heart pumps more slowly. This change causes blood pressure to drop, as the blood takes longer to travel through the body.

Low blood pressure can result in dizziness, faintness, and headaches. Poor circulation causes people with anorexia to feel cold. Anorexics sometimes wear sweaters or warm layers when other people are comfortable in lightweight clothing.

In focus: putting off puberty

Girls and boys who develop anorexia before they have entered **puberty** usually do not experience the physical changes that are associated with growing up. For example, girls do not develop breasts, and boys with anorexia do not grow body hair. When they return to healthful eating patterns, they can expect to go through the usual changes of puberty.

No more periods

As anorexic girls start to lose significant amounts of weight, they stop having periods. This is one of the body's automatic responses to inadequate nourishment. Regular periods are a sign that a woman's body is ready to bear children. The female body needs a certain amount of fat to support that function. When body fat falls below the minimum amount, the body shuts down its ability to reproduce.

Regular periods usually return once a girl resumes normal eating and reaches a healthy weight. Sometimes it takes months or even years for periods to return, and a few long-term anorexics may have problems getting pregnant. However, more than three-fourths of recovered anorexics do not experience lasting effects.

Some anorexics become so weak that they can barely walk. The body uses all available energy to power the most vital organs—the heart, brain, and lungs.

The link between eating disorders and depression is unclear. Medical professionals have noted that many patients with eating disorders have a family or personal history of depression. Some researchers think that depression may precede an eating disorder. Depression may also result in part from the feelings of loneliness and isolation that come with an eating disorder. The physical effects of an eating disorder are linked to depression, too. People with anorexia and bulimia have shortages of **hormones**, minerals, and vitamins that help to maintain an even mood.

Brittle bones and teeth

Anorexics and bulimics lack calcium and other important nutrients in their diet. Calcium is essential for building bones, especially during the teenage years. Young teenagers who develop eating disorders may fail to achieve full growth.

Long-term anorexics and bulimics are at risk of developing **osteopenia** (brittle bones). This condition can result in broken bones and in the curving of the spine in later life. About 90 percent of anorexics experience osteopenia, and 40 percent develop **osteoporosis**, more advanced loss of bone minerals.

Lack of calcium in the diet also affects the teeth, making them prone to decay. This problem is most severe for bulimics, whose teeth are damaged by the stomach acid in their vomit.

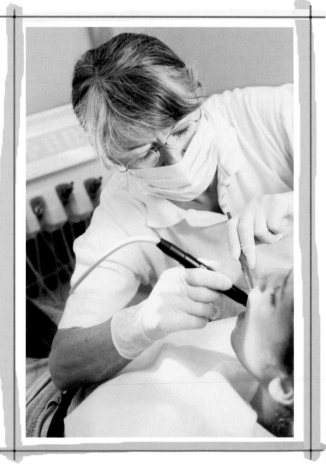

Teenagers with eating disorders may have significant tooth decay and need a lot of corrective dental work.

causes irritation to the **digestive tract**, and bulimics sometimes feel painful burning sensations in the stomach and chest. Some bulimics lose control of the gag reflex, so vomiting happens automatically every time they eat.

Digestive problems

Some teens with anorexia or bulimia suffer from intense stomach pain. As anorexics reduce their intake of food, their stomachs shrink dramatically. Eating even a small amount of food can cause discomfort and **bloating**. Some people with anorexia experience diarrhea, while others have painful constipation.

Bulimics can develop similar digestive problems as a result of abusing laxatives. Frequent laxative users have painful stomach cramps. They can also have diarrhea or constipation.

The practice of forced vomiting also results in problems. Frequent vomiting

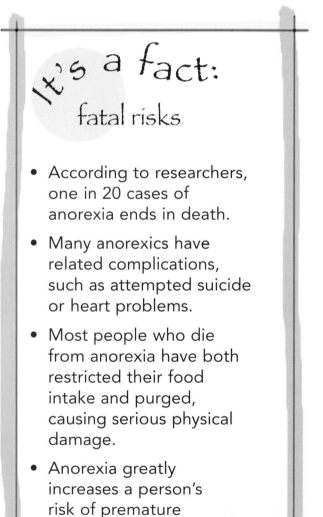

It's a fact: fatal risks

- According to researchers, one in 20 cases of anorexia ends in death.

- Many anorexics have related complications, such as attempted suicide or heart problems.

- Most people who die from anorexia have both restricted their food intake and purged, causing serious physical damage.

- Anorexia greatly increases a person's risk of premature death.

In focus: heart problems

People with anorexia put their hearts under a massive strain because they eat too little. This strain is increased if they also exercise too much. Meanwhile, the heart is deprived of essential tissue-building minerals, such as potassium and calcium, and its muscles start to waste away. People who use laxatives put their hearts in particular danger, as laxatives strip the body of almost all its potassium. Calcium and potassium are **electrolytes**, substances that are necessary to maintain a normal heartbeat. When electrolytes become imbalanced, anorexics and bulimics can experience irregular heart rhythms. In extreme cases, they can die from heart failure.

Wasting muscles

As anorexia becomes advanced, muscles (especially in the upper arms and the legs) weaken and waste away. The damage is caused partly by a lack of potassium and other important minerals. Also, once the body has used up all its reserves of fat for energy, it starts to break down muscle tissue instead.

Damaged organs

Anorexia and bulimia can have harmful effects on all body organs. People with

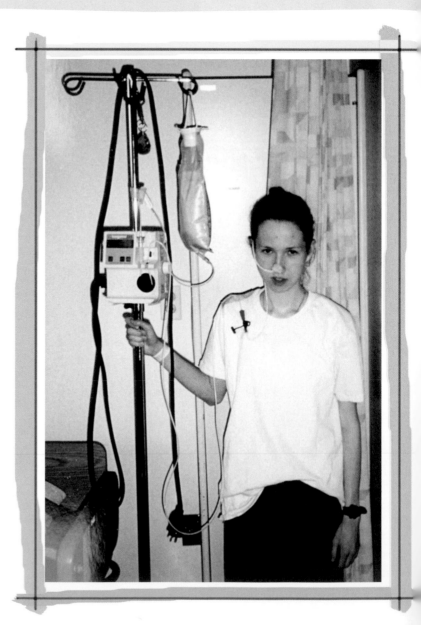

Some anorexics must be treated in a hospital, where fluids are given to provide the essential minerals their bodies need.

these eating disorders generally lack essential minerals, such as potassium and sodium. This shortage can seriously weaken and damage their organs. Imbalances in blood sugar levels can stop the liver from functioning properly. Repeated use of laxatives and diuretics causes dehydration, which can result in serious damage to the kidneys. Meanwhile, the nervous system ceases to function properly. Complex thinking and concentration become increasingly difficult as too little oxygen reaches the brain.

A fatal combination

Approximately one in 20 anorexics dies from the condition or its complications. In a small percentage of this group, the cause of death is heart or liver failure. However, the majority of deaths result from a combination of factors. As their disease progresses, anorexics become progressively weaker and develop more serious physical problems. At the same time, depression often worsens. Some people with advanced eating disorders commit suicide.

CASE STUDY

Mariel developed anorexia when she was 12. For the next six years, she survived mainly on salad, rice cakes, and diet soda. Occasionally, she would allow herself to eat larger amounts or different foods, but then she always purged, forcing herself to vomit. Mariel also abused laxatives and diuretics. Even though she felt very weak, she exercised for two to three hours a day.

At the age of 18, Mariel looked like a desperately ill 10-year-old. Her arms and legs were stick thin, with wasted muscles. Her joints and her stomach were swollen. She had early signs of liver failure, and she often experienced dizziness and irregular heart rhythms. Mariel had been in and out of treatment centers, but each time she left, she began restricting food and overexercising again.

By her 18th birthday, Mariel was so weak that she was forced to spend most of her time resting. Still, she continued starving herself and pushing herself to work out. A week later, she experienced heart failure. Just as her former classmates were graduating and beginning their adult lives, Mariel died.

Chapter 5: *What causes eating disorders?*

What causes teenagers to become anorexic or to develop bulimia? What makes some young people binge or overeat compulsively? Sometimes it is hard to find the answers to these questions. Teenagers who struggle with food have their own individual situations, challenges, and personality types. However, many young people face similar pressures that can contribute to the development of eating disorders.

Under pressure

Eating disorders generally develop as a response to pressure or stress. Everyone has to deal with pressure, but stresses can be especially intense at certain times in a person's life. As young people approach the teenage years, many of them have trouble

As children become teenagers, they start to look at themselves in a new way. A few feel unhappy with what they see and decide to make changes.

Taking control

Faced with all these stresses, some teens feel that their lives are out of control. They may turn to food as an area where they can take control by making their own decisions about what and how much they eat. Other teenagers see food as a form of escape or comfort, and they start to binge or overeat.

coping with the pressures brought on by multiple physical and emotional changes.

Girls and boys in their early teens face stresses at school. In middle school and high school, classwork and exams become increasingly demanding. Some teenagers come into conflict with their parents or other adults as they try out their new independence. Teens may also feel pressure from their friends—to keep up with the latest fashions and to be popular with the opposite sex.

Some teens experience pressure from all sides—their parents, their teachers, and even their friends. These stresses can contribute to the development of an eating disorder.

In focus: teens at risk

Two groups of teens are especially likely to develop eating disorders. Teenagers who already have serious problems, such as drug addiction or family conflict, are especially vulnerable. Other teens at risk are perfectionists—people who appear on the surface to be successful and confident but who have always pushed themselves because they fear failure.

Perfectionists set very high standards for everything they do, and they blame themselves whenever they fall short. As teenagers, they face new challenges that can make them feel anxious and self-critical. Some teens respond to these pressures by turning to extreme dieting as a way of testing themselves or being "the best" at something.

Diet dangers

One of the major stresses faced by teenagers is the pressure to be thin. Everywhere they look—in magazines and newspapers and on TV—they see criticism of people who are overweight. They also see advertisements for diets that are supposed to change people's lives. The message given out by the media is loud and clear: If you want to be happy, popular, and successful, you need to be slim.

Once girls start to develop curves, they become even more aware of their bodies and of media pressure to be thin. At this stage, many girls become very critical of their own shape or size. Some of them decide that life would be much better if only they were very slim, and they start to diet. A growing number of teenage boys feel pressured to have a lean and muscular body, so they decide to take control of what they eat.

Peer pressure

Media pressure is not the only influence that drives people to diet. Teenagers also experience pressure from their peers. If they are overweight, they may face teasing and cruel remarks. Sometimes the pressure is less direct. For example, girls may hear their friends talking frequently about diets. They may notice that some girls are slimmer than they are. These experiences can push teens to diet.

Super-thin celebrities

Today's magazines are full of photographs of super-thin celebrities. Many actresses and fashion models are also extremely thin, with almost childlike bodies. Many models may be

Magazines often use altered photographs of models and celebrities that make the women look thinner than they actually are. These images can mislead readers and portray an unrealistic ideal of beauty.

naturally slim, but most of them admit they have to diet strenuously to stay so thin. Some have spoken openly about their struggles with anorexia or bulimia. In 2006 and 2007, three South American models died from complications of anorexia. Their deaths prompted debate in the fashion industry about the use of "size-zero" models.

Even though articles in the media point to the dangers of being very underweight, teenage girls are still confronted by many images of super-skinny models, actresses, and celebrities. They usually dress in expensive clothes and look glamorous, so it's not surprising that many teens dream of being as thin as these women.

In focus: the super-skinny debate

Recently, some groups have campaigned to ban ultra-thin models from magazines and fashion show runways. In response, a few designers have agreed not to employ models who are unhealthily thin. However, some members of the fashion industry have resisted such a ban.

Images of super-skinny models sometimes make healthy teenagers feel self-conscious about their size. It can be hard for teens to accept their own appearance, when they are surrounded by images of models, actresses, and celebrities who are very thin.

Sports pressures

Teenagers who want to excel at sports need to be physically fit. They have to put in many hours of training to keep their bodies in peak condition. Sometimes they even need to maintain a certain weight. Dancers and gymnasts are usually expected to stay extremely slim. Wrestlers and boxers have to control their weight to stay within various categories or classes, such as flyweight and middleweight.

Some young people respond to the pressures of their sport by depriving themselves of certain foods or by putting themselves on a very strict diet. At the same time, they may increase the hours they spend in training. These can be the first steps on the path to a serious eating disorder.

Boys and eating disorders

A growing number of teenage boys are experiencing eating disorders. Today, one in ten people with an eating disorder is male.

Some boys are binge eaters or compulsive overeaters. Others

Teenagers who train as ballet dancers or gymnasts are under great pressure to stay slim. Most of them eat healthfully, but a few respond to the pressure by cutting down on food in an unhealthy way.

develop anorexia or bulimia. Teenage boys may develop anorexia after they have been teased about their weight. Or they may simply decide that they want their bodies to look lean and toned.

Boys have less body fat than girls do, so an eating disorder such as anorexia can go unnoticed longer. By the time the problem is recognized, the individual is often in urgent need of help.

Boys can feel much pressure as girls do to change the way they look.

CASE STUDY

Tony was a shy, chubby boy who had always felt awkward about his body. He never took off his shirt, even on the hottest days. He didn't enjoy swimming because he felt that everyone was laughing at him. One day he made a decision: He would start a workout program, and he'd stick to it until he had a lean, toned body like those of the athletes he admired.

Tony soon discovered that trying to have the perfect body was very hard work. He got up early to run and work out with weights before school. Yet he still felt that he was too fat. So he decided to cut back on food as well. Once Tony started dieting, he soon noticed a difference—and his family did, too. His parents began to worry that Tony was losing too much weight. They also found that he had become moody, withdrawn, and irritable.

Even though Tony had changed his body shape, his life at school didn't improve. In fact, he thought that people were looking at him strangely. Still, he was determined not to give up everything he had achieved. He pushed himself even harder, eating less and exercising more. When he collapsed from exhaustion and dehydration, his friends and family finally recognized the severity of his illness.

Escape from the adult world

There are many factors that can cause anorexia. Some teenagers with the disorder describe their wish to stop their bodies from maturing. Having a childlike body can seem very appealing to teens who seek to escape the choices and responsibilities of the adult world. For example, a teenage girl may want to look like a child as a way to avoid the pressures of dating and the unwanted attention of boys.

Sexual abuse

In a few cases, teenagers develop anorexia or other eating disorders after a **trauma**, such as **sexual abuse**. That kind of experience can make the victims feel frightened of their sexuality or ashamed of their bodies. As they struggle with their negative feelings about sex, some teens react by overeating as a way of giving themselves comfort. Others may develop a destructive pattern of bingeing and purging in response to their sense of disgust at their bodies. Some teenagers develop anorexia as they seek to retreat into the safety of childhood.

Extra pressures

Some young people run a high risk of developing eating disorders because of the serious problems they face in their daily lives. These troubled teens may come from homes where constant conflict or even violence

Some troubled teenagers feel unhappy about joining the adult world. To them, it seems safer to stay a child. By losing a lot of weight, they make their bodies child-like. However, they create a whole new set of problems for themselves.

occurs. They may have parents who are struggling with addiction or illness.

Other teens may experience depression or be involved in crime. Some abuse alcohol or drugs. Teenagers faced with problems like these can feel that their lives are dangerously out of control. In these circumstances, some of them are desperate for a way to regain control over some part of their lives. Sadly, some of them develop eating disorders as they seek to cope with the difficult problems they face.

A family link?

Research shows that a tendency to eating disorders may be passed down from one generation to another. Teens who have a parent or sibling with an eating disorder are at increased risk.

Teenagers learn their eating habits from their parents. A child whose parent is overly concerned with dieting is more likely to develop an eating problem than a child who is brought up in a family where all members eat healthfully.

In focus: eating disorders, East and West

Until recently, anorexia and bulimia were much more common among people living in western Europe and the United States than in Asian countries. However, that situation is changing. Over the last ten years, Japan, Korea, and China have experienced a dramatic rise in the numbers of people with eating disorders.

In Japan, the percentage of anorexics increased tenfold between 1980 and 2000. Some experts say the increase is partly the result of the influence of Western movies, television, and magazines.

The number of people with eating disorders is rising sharply in Japan and other countries in Asia.

Chapter 6: *Getting help*

It is possible for people to make a complete recovery from an eating disorder. However, they usually can't get better on their own. Fortunately, plenty of people and organizations are available to provide help.

Recognizing the problem

The first and most significant step on the road to recovery is to recognize the problem. Denial, by both young patients and their families, is the main reason that eating disorders progress without being treated. Once teenagers admit that they have difficulties with eating, they have made the first move in breaking away from unhealthy patterns of thinking and eating.

At this stage, it's important to seek outside help. Teenagers can talk to a parent, a school counselor, or a friend, who can help them get in touch with a health professional. Some teens choose to call a helpline or visit a specialized web site. Many organizations provide educational materials, expert referrals, and information on treatment options. (See page 47.)

Many teens find that talking to an experienced therapist about their difficulties with food is a great relief. They feel that they are finally able to honestly discuss the problems that have been worrying them.

Finding expert help

The first source for medical advice can be a teenager's doctor. Some family physicians treat eating disorders, but many refer their patients to a specialized doctor or clinic. Psychiatrists, **therapists**, and **nutritionists** can also help.

Therapists who specialize in eating disorders look at the reasons underlying their patients' problems with food. Therapists also help people change their perceptions about body image and assist patients in developing healthy eating patterns.

It's a fact:

long-term outcomes

- Approximately half of all anorexics and bulimics make a full recovery.
- About 30 percent make a partial recovery.
- About 20 percent experience no substantial improvement.
- On average, anorexia lasts 1.7 years.
- The average duration of bulimia is 8.3 years.

Teenagers with eating disorders may also get specific advice on diet and nutrition. Nutritionists discuss with patients how much they should eat to stay healthy. Nutritionists also explain the kinds of foods that teens need to eat regularly to get proper amounts of essential minerals and vitamins.

Sometimes young people with eating disorders need immediate medical attention for serious health problems caused by the disorder. Once the patients resume healthful eating habits, many of the physical effects are reversed.

Nutritionists give advice on how to achieve and maintain a healthy body weight.

Starting therapy

Therapy for eating disorders may
include regular sessions with a
therapist. These sessions can help
young people understand more about
why and how the disorder started.
Therapists can also help teens change
the things in their lives that made
them turn to food to gain control or
seek comfort.

One of the most important elements
in recovery is the development of
greater self-esteem, so therapists work
hard at helping their patients value
themselves more. Once teenagers have
a better sense of self-worth and truly

*Regular therapy can help teenagers
develop greater self-esteem and make
changes to restore healthy eating habits.*

want to be healthy, they can more
easily return to normal eating patterns.

Most therapy takes place in one-to-one
sessions, but sometimes small groups
of people with similar problems are
treated together. In group therapy,
participants can share their thoughts
and feelings, and support one another
in the effort to get well.

Sometimes, family members take part
in therapy sessions, with the young
person's permission. Therapists may

also meet with parents separately. In these sessions, therapists help parents understand the possible causes of their children's eating disorders. Therapists also suggest ways in which families can help teenagers recover.

Taking one step at a time

Recovery from an eating disorder can take weeks, months, or even years. During this period, a young person may experience many setbacks. Therapists encourage their patients to take small steps toward normal eating and not to expect too much from themselves right away.

Teenagers who are recovering from eating disorders occasionally slip back into unhealthy patterns. Therapists urge their patients not to feel disheartened and remind them of the progress they have made.

In focus: keeping a diary

Many therapists encourage their patients to keep a diary. This journal should be an honest record of everything they eat. It should also include notes about the teen's changing moods and thoughts.

Writing a diary can help recovering teenagers face up to their eating habits. Once they see their food intake written on paper, they realize how little (or how much) they are eating.

The diary also helps people recognize the link between their thoughts and emotions and what they are eating. As teenagers work at returning to normal eating patterns, a journal can help chart their progress.

Keeping a journal or a diary can help teenagers sort out complex emotions.

CASE STUDY

Jade, an anorexic, weighed less than 70 pounds (32 kilograms) when she was admitted to a hospital. She was dangerously weak and dehydrated. She was given fluids intravenously for the first two days. Then she was fed through a tube into her stomach until her weight reached a safer level. Once she was strong enough, Jade was encouraged to eat, starting with very small amounts of food. Hospital staff monitored her food and gave her plenty of support and encouragement. Jade made good progress, and within a few weeks she was able to leave the hospital and go to a residential treatment program.

At the clinic, Jade had regular individual sessions with a therapist. She also joined group sessions with other anorexics. They discussed their problems with food and gave each other support. For the first time, Jade felt that she was able to talk freely about her eating disorder. At the same time, Jade's parents received counseling sessions. The therapist explained ways the parents could help their daughter return to a healthy weight and a normal pattern of eating.

In the supportive atmosphere of the clinic, Jade made a very good recovery. Although she sometimes felt tempted to return to her disordered eating behaviors, most days she just felt lucky to be well and strong again.

Serious cases

Some teenagers with eating disorders put themselves in serious physical danger. They may have heart problems or other damaged organs, such as kidneys or livers. In these cases, patients have to be admitted to a hospital where they can get emergency treatment for their medical problems.

Anorexics who have become dangerously thin and weak may need to be fed **intravenously**

Some teens struggle with eating problems for years. They need support to help them return to healthy eating patterns.

(through a vein) or through a tube directly into the stomach. Once they have gained enough strength to feed themselves, they are encouraged to eat small amounts of food at frequent, regular intervals. Because the patients' stomachs have shrunk dramatically, food must be introduced gradually, slowly building up to normal-sized meals.

A tragic end

Sadly, not everyone with an eating disorder makes a full recovery. Some people struggle with eating disorders throughout their lives. They become increasingly weak and can die early from a range of causes—severe malnourishment, organ failure, a heart attack, or suicide.

Some teens who have been extremely ill are able to make a full recovery. They may benefit from regular meetings with support groups.

Chapter 7: *Staying well*

A large proportion of teenagers with eating disorders make a full recovery. After a period of struggling with food, they manage to establish healthy eating patterns. What can teenagers do to help themselves stay well, and how can they avoid developing destructive eating patterns?

Eating healthfully

Whether someone feels tempted to eat too much or too little, the best way to beat those feelings is to establish a pattern of regular, healthful meals. Skipping meals is never a good idea. It can easily lead to overeating at the next meal.

It is best to limit foods such as cakes and cookies, which fill you up quickly but soon leave you feeling hungry again. Instead, try to eat foods that provide a steady release of energy to keep you going until the next meal. Most foods that release energy slowly are high in **fiber**, so they take longer to digest. They include fresh fruits and vegetables, whole-grain bread, brown rice, and whole-grain pasta.

Eating a diet that is rich in fresh fruits and vegetables gives you energy. Along with regular exercise, these foods help keep your body in good condition.

Avoiding diets

Young people should avoid dieting unless they are **clinically overweight** and have been advised by a doctor to lose weight. Low-calorie diets disturb the body's natural functions. These diets may bring rapid weight loss, but most of it is water and muscle mass, not fat. You will feel too tired to focus on schoolwork or keep up with other activities. Plus, experts say that severe dieting can trigger anorexia, bulimia, or other eating disorders.

People come in all shapes and sizes. Since the recent deaths of several models from complications of anorexia, many people have reacted strongly against the fashion industry's ideal of unnatural thinness. Most

In focus: *taking action!*

If you think that you are developing unusual eating patterns—or if you are worried about one of your friends—take action now. Talk to someone you know and trust about your concerns. See page 47 for a list of organizations and people to contact for help.

people think that women and girls who are at a healthy weight for their height look strong, fit, and attractive.

Having energy for life

During the teenage years you need plenty of energy. You should get that energy by eating healthful meals, exercising regularly, and getting plenty of sleep. If you have a healthy lifestyle, you will feel and look your best. Then you can get on with enjoying your life and accomplishing your goals.

Eating shouldn't cause stress or worry. Sharing food can be one of life's pleasures.

Glossary

anorexia nervosa: an eating disorder in which people feel an overwhelming need to be thin. Anorexics usually have a distorted body image, abnormal eating patterns, malnutrition, and excessive weight loss.

binge-eating disorder: an eating disorder in which people eat a large amount of food in a short time without purging or fasting afterward

bingeing: eating a very large amount of food within a short time

bloating: swelling of the stomach, caused by air trapped inside the intestines

blood vessels: tubes through which blood circulates within the body

body image: a person's mental picture of his or her body

bulimia nervosa: an eating disorder in which people binge on large amounts of food and then try to empty their bodies of the food, usually by vomiting or taking laxatives

calories: units used for measuring the amount of energy provided by a food

circulation: the movement of blood throughout the body

clinically overweight: so overweight that health is in serious danger

compulsive eating disorder: an eating disorder in which people feel an overwhelming need to eat more food, even when they are full

dehydration: the loss of water from the body

depression: a mood disorder marked by persistent sadness, inactivity, difficulty in concentration, a significant increase or decrease in appetite and sleep, and feelings of hopelessness

diabetes: an illness in which people have high levels of sugar in the blood

digestive tract: the tube that extends from the mouth to the large intestine. It includes the esophagus, stomach, gallbladder, liver, and pancreas.

diuretic: causing an increase in the flow of urine

electrolytes: substances in the body fluids, such as calcium, sodium, and potassium. Proper balance of electrolytes is important for muscle coordination, heart activity, and concentration.

fast: to go without food for long periods of time

fiber: the parts of some foods, such as cereals and fresh fruits and vegetables, that pass through the body without being digested

gag reflex: a natural reaction to stimulation of tissue at the back of the throat. It brings about vomiting.

hormones: chemicals formed in the body that control functions such as growth, development, and reproduction

intravenously: by way of the veins

lanugo: fine, downy hair that grows on the face and body of anorexics to help conserve heat

laxatives: substances that cause people to expel solid wastes from their bodies

nutrients: the parts of food that nourish the body

nutritionists: experts on food and its use by the body

obsessive-compulsive disorder (OCD): a mental illness marked by unreasonable fears or uncontrollable thoughts. People with OCD often feel a strong need to perform repeated actions, such as counting or handwashing.

osteopenia: low bone density

osteoporosis: decreased bone mass and density, producing porous and fragile bones

perfectionists: people who seek or demand perfection, usually to an unreasonable degree

protein: a substance found in some foods, such as eggs, milk, cheese, meat, and fish, that helps bodies grow and repair themselves

psychological: relating to the mind and the emotions

puberty: a series of physical changes that marks the end of childhood and the start of sexual maturity

purging: getting rid of food from the body, usually by vomiting or taking laxatives

salivary glands: organs in the cheeks that produce saliva to aid in digestion

self-esteem: confidence and satisfaction in oneself

sexual abuse: physical or sexual contact with a person against his or her will

therapists: people who are specially trained to give help, support, and advice to others

trauma: an event or experience that is very upsetting and shocking

Further information

Books to read

Bowman, Grace. *Thin*. New York: Penguin, 2007.

Kingsley, Jo, and Alice Kingsley. *Alice in the Looking Glass: A Mother and Daughter's Experience of Anorexia*. London: Piatkus, 2005.

Pettit, Christie. *Empty: A Story of Anorexia*. Grand Rapids, Mich.: Baker Publishing Group, 2006.

Sparks, Beatrice. *Kim: Empty Inside: The Diary of an Anonymous Teenager*. New York: HarperCollins, 2002.

Organizations to contact

National Eating Disorders Association (NEDA)
Web site: **www.nationaleatingdisorders.org**
Toll-free helpline: 1-800-931-2237
Helpline volunteers provide support services and guidance to people struggling with eating disorders, their families, and their friends. The helpline is open Monday to Friday, 8:30 A.M. to 4:30 P.M. Pacific time.

National Association of Anorexia Nervosa and Associated Disorders (ANAD)
Web site: **www.anad.org**
Hotline: 847-831-3438
Volunteers answer thousands of hotline calls each year, helping individuals and their families find resources and providing referrals to professionals. The hotline is open Monday to Friday, 9 A.M. to 5 P.M. Central time.

Helpful web sites

Anorexia Nervosa and Related Eating Disorders, Inc. (ANRED)
www.anred.com
ANRED's web site provides detailed information on anorexia nervosa, bulimia nervosa, binge eating, and other eating disorders. The site also includes advice for recovery and prevention.

Harris Center for Education and Advocacy in Eating Disorders
www.harriscentermgh.org
The Harris Center at Massachusetts General Hospital works to research, treat, and prevent eating disorders. The web site includes relevant information, resources, and advice for family and friends.

TeensHealth
www.kidshealth.org/teen/your_mind/ mental_health/eat_disorder.html
TeensHealth (part of the KidsHealth web site) offers young people and families accurate, current information developed by doctors and other health experts.

Center for Young Women's Health
www.youngwomenshealth.org/ eating_disorders.html
Affiliated with the Division of Adolescent/Young Adult Medicine at Children's Hospital Boston, the center offers information on eating disorders for teens, family members, and close friends.

Index